Aha Grammar 3

Workbook

Happy House

CoNTeNTs

Chapter 1 Articles & Quantifiers

Chapter 2 Past Simple Tense: Be Verbs

Chapter 3 Past Simple Tense: Verbs

Chapter 4 Future Tense

Chapter 5 Adverbs

Chapter 6 Wh- Questions

UNIT 01 Articles

GRAMMAR POINT

부정관사 a/an

- 부정관사 a/an은 '하나의'라는 뜻을 나타내며 셀 수 있는 단수명사 앞에 사용합니다.
- 자음(모음을 제외한 나머지 음가)으로 시작되는 명사 앞에는 a를 붙입니다.
- 모음(a, e, i, o, u)으로 시작되는 명사 앞에는 an을 붙입니다.
- 복수명사 앞에는 부정관사 a/an을 붙이지 않습니다.

정관사 the

- 정관사 the는 앞에서 말한 명사를 다시 언급할 때나 세상에서 하나뿐인 사물 앞에 붙입니다.

a / an	any one thing (불특정한 하나의 것)	a book	a cat	an ostrich
zero	more than two things (두 개 이상의 것들)	✗ pencils	✗ girls	✗ apples
the	specific thing(s) (특정한 것(들))	the book	the ostrich	the pencils
	one and only thing (유일한 것)	the sun	the moon	the sky

A Look and check.

1

It is ☐ a ostrich.
 ✓ an ostrich.

2

It is ☐ a sun.
☐ the sun.

3

They are ☐ balloons.
☐ a balloons.

4

They are ☐ pencils.
☐ a pencils.

5

It is ☐ a moon.
☐ the moon.

6
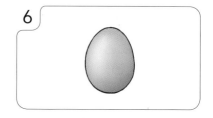
It is ☐ eggs.
☐ an egg.

4

B Read and write *a*, *an*, *the*, or *X*.

1 You have __X__ mirrors. __The__ mirrors are round.

2 There is _____ fish. _____ fish is blue.

3 It is _____ octopus. _____ octopus is red.

4 It is _____ moon. _____ moon is yellow.

5 There are _____ puppies. _____ puppies are cute.

6 He has _____ bike. _____ bike is new.

C Read, write, and match.

1 Look at __the__ sky.
__The__ sky is blue.

2 She has _____ apple.
_____ apple is red.

3 I have _____ book.
_____ book is fun.

4 Look at _____ Earth.
_____ Earth is round.

5 They have _____ car.
_____ car is new.

6 He has _____ pets.
_____ pets are a dog and a cat.

D Read and unscramble.

1 [a] [is] [There] [chair.] The chair is brown.

→ <u>There is a chair.</u>

2 Look at the sun. [sun] [is] [The] [bright.]

→ _____

3 [is] [ant.] [an] [There] The ant is black.

→ _____

4 I have ships. [ships] [The] [are] [white.]

→ _____

5 [is] [There] [an] [elephant.] The elephant is big.

→ _____

E Read and correct.

1 It is the Earth. A Earth is round.

→ <u>It is the Earth. The Earth is round.</u>

2 There are a alligators. The alligators are scary.

→ _____

3 There is a balloon. A balloon is blue.

→ _____

4 You have an pencil. The pencil is short.

→ _____

5 He has an oranges. The oranges are sweet.

→ _____

Some / Any

GRAMMAR POINT

수량 형용사 Some / Any

- some과 any는 '약간의' 라는 뜻을 나타냅니다.
- some과 any 뒤에는 셀 수 있는 명사의 복수형 또는 셀 수 없는 명사가 옵니다.
- some은 긍정문에 사용합니다.
- any는 부정문과 의문문에 사용합니다.

	Some / Any + Countable Noun	Some / Any + Uncountable Noun
Affirmative (긍정문)	I have some apples. (저는 약간의 사과를 가지고 있습니다.) I have some grapes. (저는 약간의 포도를 가지고 있습니다.)	I have some bread. (저는 약간의 빵을 가지고 있습니다.) I have some cheese. (저는 약간의 치즈를 가지고 있습니다.)
Negative (부정문)	I don't have any apples. (저는 사과를 가지고 있지 않습니다.) I don't have any grapes. (저는 포도를 가지고 있지 않습니다.)	I don't have any bread. (저는 빵을 가지고 있지 않습니다.) I don't have any cheese. (저는 치즈를 가지고 있지 않습니다.)
Question (의문문)	Do you have any apples? (당신은 사과를 가지고 있습니까?) Do you have any grapes? (당신은 포도를 가지고 있습니까?)	Do you have any bread? (당신은 빵을 가지고 있습니까?) Do you have any cheese? (당신은 치즈를 가지고 있습니까?)

A Look and circle.

1  There is ⟨some⟩ / any water.

2  There aren't some / any flowers.

3  Do you have some / any toys?

Yes, we do.

B Read and write *some* or *any*.

1 Is there _____ any _____ chocolate?

   Yes, there is _____ some _____ chocolate.

2 Do you have _____ pens?

   No, I don't have _____ pens. But I have _____ pencils.

3 Does she have _____ milk?

   No, she doesn't have _____ milk. But she has _____ yogurt.

4 Are there _____ toys?

   Yes, there are _____ toys.

5 Is there _____ cake?

   No, there isn't _____ cake. But there is _____ pie.

C Look and write using *some* or *any*.

milk
apples
cheese
donuts
bread
grapes
ice cream
crackers

1 He has _____ some _____ apples _____.

2 He doesn't have _____ _____.

3 He has _____ _____.

4 Does he have _____ _____? No, he doesn't.

5 They have _____ _____.

6 They don't have _____ _____.

7 They have _____ _____.

8 Do they have _____ _____? No, they don't.

D Read and unscramble.

1 [notebooks.] [don't] [any] [I] [have]

→ _I don't have any notebooks._

2 [any] [there] [pencils?] [Are]

→ _____

3 [doesn't] [have] [butter.] [any] [He]

→ _____

4 [juice?] [Is] [there] [any]

→ _____

5 [They] [bread.] [some] [have]

→ _____

6 [hot dogs.] [There] [are] [some]

→ _____

E Read and correct.

1 There aren't any money. → _There isn't any money._

2 There are some eraser. → _____

3 Does he have some rulers? → _____

4 I have any rice. → _____

5 There aren't some cars. → _____

6 Is there any cheeses? → _____

Many / Much / a Lot of

GRAMMAR POINT

수량형용사 Many / Much / a Lot of

- many/much/a lot of 는 '많은' 이라는 의미를 가집니다.
- many 뒤에는 셀 수 있는 명사의 복수형이 옵니다.
- much 뒤에는 셀 수 없는 명사가 오며, much는 긍정문에서는 잘 쓰이지 않습니다.
- a lot of 뒤에는 셀 수 있는 명사의 복수형이나 셀 수 없는 명사 둘 다 올 수 있습니다.

	Many + Countable Noun	Much + Uncountable Noun
Affirmative (긍정문)	There are many / a lot of books. (책이 많이 있습니다.) There are many / a lot of pencils. (연필이 많이 있습니다.)	There is a lot of water. (물이 많이 있습니다.) There is a lot of juice. (주스가 많이 있습니다.)
Negative (부정문)	There aren't many / a lot of books. (책이 많이 있지 않습니다.) There aren't many / a lot of pencils. (연필이 많이 있지 않습니다.)	There isn't much / a lot of water. (물이 많이 있지 않습니다.) There isn't much / a lot of juice. (주스가 많이 있지 않습니다.)
Question (의문문)	Are there many / a lot of books? (책이 많이 있습니까?) Are there many / a lot of pencils? (연필이 많이 있습니까?)	Is there much / a lot of water? (물이 많이 있습니까?) Is there much / a lot of juice? (주스가 많이 있습니까?)

A Read and write.

orange	sugar	chocolate	leaf	bread	puppy
juice	car	butter	dish	ice cream	child

Many		Much	
oranges			

B **Read and circle.**

1 Is there [many / **much**] water?

2 She has [many / much] crayons.

3 There aren't [much / a lot of] students.

4 I don't have [many / much] honey.

5 Are there [many / much] balls?

6 Does he have [many / a lot of] cheese?

C **Look and write using** *many*, *much*, **or** *a lot of*.

| cheese | salt | cookies | pencils | sugar | strawberries |

1 There are ___many___ ___cookies___ .
= There are ___a lot of___ ___cookies___ .

2 There isn't _____ _____ .
= There isn't _____ _____ .

3 Are there _____ _____ ?
= Are there _____ _____ ?

4 He has _____ _____ .

5 She doesn't have _____ _____ .
= She doesn't have _____ _____ .

6 Do you have _____ _____ ?
= Do you have _____ _____ ?

D Read and unscramble.

1
| a lot of | There | chocolate. | is |

→ <u>There is a lot of chocolate.</u>

2
| There | much | isn't | oil. |

→ _____

3
| are | many | There | birds. |

→ _____

4
| sugar? | Is | much | there |

→ _____

5
| crayons. | a lot of | There | aren't |

→ _____

6
| many | Are | there | students? |

→ _____

E Read and correct.

1 There aren't much people. → <u>There aren't many people.</u>

2 Is there many juice? → _____

3 There is many forks. → _____

4 There aren't a lot of butter. → _____

5 There is a lot of lemonades. → _____

6 Are there many balloon? → _____

Units 1-3

A **Read and write *a*, *an*, *the*, or *X*.**

1 She has ____a____ doll. ____The____ doll is pretty.

2 I have _____ umbrella. _____ umbrella is red.

3 Look at _____ sky. _____ sky is gray.

4 There are _____ pictures on the wall. _____ pictures are nice.

5 There is _____ kite on the tree. _____ kite is blue.

6 They have _____ bikes. _____ bikes are new.

B **Look and write.**

| some   any | rulers   water   butter   toys   money   flowers |

1
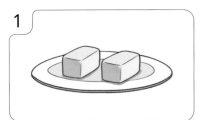
There is ___some___
___butter___.

2

There aren't _____
_____.

3

They have _____
_____.

4

I don't have _____
_____.

5

Does he have _____
_____?

6
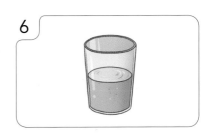
Is there _____
_____?

C Look and write *many*, *much*, **or** *a lot of*.

1 Are there _____many_____ flowers?

= Are there _____a lot of_____ flowers?

2 There isn't _____ bread.

= There isn't _____ bread.

3 There are _____ books.

= There are _____ books.

4 Is there _____ rice?

= Is there _____ rice?

5 There is _____ water.

D Read, circle, and write.

1 There is ____a____ tree. ____The____ tree is tall.

ⓐ a, The   ⓑ an, A   ⓒ X, The

2 I have _____ balloons. _____ balloons are blue.

ⓐ a, The   ⓑ an, A   ⓒ X, The

3 He has _____ robots. He doesn't have _____ dolls.

ⓐ any, some   ⓑ some, any   ⓒ some, some

4 Is there _____ juice? Yes, there is.

ⓐ a   ⓑ many   ⓒ much

5 There are _____ cars on the street.

ⓐ a   ⓑ many   ⓒ much

Past Simple: Be Verbs (Affirmatives)

GRAMMAR POINT

Be동사 과거시제 (긍정문)

- Be동사의 과거형은 was, were가 있으며 '~이었다' 또는 '~있었다'라고 해석합니다.
- Be동사 am, is의 과거형은 was이고, be동사 are의 과거형은 were입니다.
- 과거의 사실이나 상태를 말할 때 사용하고, yesterday, last week 등과 같은 과거 시간 부사와 함께 사용합니다.

Affirmative	
Was	**Were**
I He She was happy. It	We You were happy. They
(저는 / 그는 / 그녀는 / 그것은 행복했습니다.)	(우리는 / 당신(들)은 / 그들은 행복했습니다.)

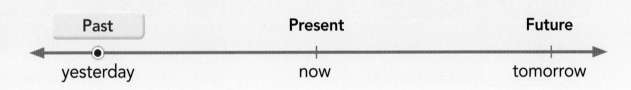

Past — yesterday   Present — now   Future — tomorrow

A Read and match.

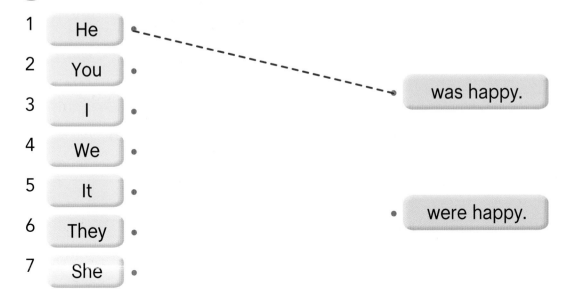

1 He
2 You
3 I
4 We
5 It
6 They
7 She

was happy.

were happy.

B Read and write *was* or *were*.

1 You ___were___ at home yesterday.

2 It _____ cloudy this morning.

3 They _____ at the library this afternoon.

4 We _____ at the theater last Sunday.

5 I _____ hungry yesterday.

6 He _____ busy last night.

C Look and write.

am	are	is	was	were

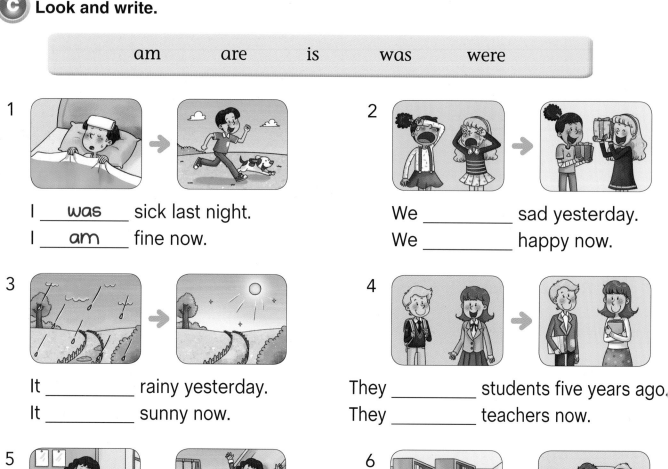

1 I ___was___ sick last night.
I ___am___ fine now.

2 We _____ sad yesterday.
We _____ happy now.

3 It _____ rainy yesterday.
It _____ sunny now.

4 They _____ students five years ago.
They _____ teachers now.

5 She _____ in the classroom this morning.
She _____ on the playground now.

6 You _____ at the library two hours ago
You _____ at home now.

D Read and unscramble.

1 [was] [She] [last night.] [thirsty]

➡ She was thirsty last night.

2 [at the shopping mall] [last Monday.] [were] [They]

➡ _____

3 [windy] [was] [It] [this morning.]

➡ _____

4 [many cookies] [were] [There] [on the dish.]

➡ _____

5 [in the bowl.] [There] [some ice cream] [was]

➡ _____

6 [last Sunday.] [were] [You] [at the theater]

➡ _____

E Read and correct.

1 We was at home yesterday. ➡ We were at home yesterday.

2 He is tired last night. ➡ _____

3 I were at the party last Sunday. ➡ _____

4 It is rainy last weekend. ➡ _____

5 She were angry yesterday. ➡ _____

6 There are many cars this morning. ➡ _____

Past Simple: Be Verbs (Negatives)

GRAMMAR PoInT

Be동사 과거시제 (부정문)

- Be동사 과거시제의 부정문은 was, were 뒤에 not을 붙여서 주어 + was/were + not 순으로 쓰고, '~아니었다' 또는 '~없었다'라고 해석합니다.
- Be동사의 과거형 + not을 줄여서 was not → wasn't, were not → weren't로 쓸 수 있습니다.
- 과거의 사실이나 상태를 말할 때 사용하고, yesterday, last week 등과 같은 과거 시간 부사와 함께 사용합니다.

Negative	
Wasn't	**Weren't**
I He She wasn't happy. It	We You weren't happy. They
(저는 / 그는 / 그녀는 / 그것은 행복하지 않았습니다.)	(우리는 / 당신(들)은 / 그들은 행복하지 않았습니다.)

* wasn't = was not, weren't = were not

A Read and circle.

1 You   was not / **were not**   hungry.

2 I   was not / were not   sad yesterday.

3 She   wasn't / weren't   at school last Monday.

4 They   wasn't / weren't   doctors before.

5 It   was not / were not   rainy yesterday.

6 We   was not / were not   rich last year.

7 You   wasn't / weren't   fine last night.

8 He   wasn't / weren't   at the museum.

B **Read and write.**

Present	Past

1 I am not sick. → I __was__ __not__ sick yesterday.

2 We are not at home. → We _____ _____ at home last night.

3 She is not tired. → She _____ _____ tired this morning.

4 They aren't at the park. → They _____ at the park yesterday.

5 There isn't any juice. → There _____ any juice this afternoon.

6 There aren't many birds. → There _____ many birds yesterday.

C **Look and write.**

1  You ___weren't___ at the park yesterday.

You ___were___ at the hospital yesterday.

2  He _____ hungry this afternoon.

He _____ thirsty this afternoon.

3  We _____ at school last weekend.

We _____ at the museum last weekend.

4  I _____ a dancer ten years ago.

I _____ a singer ten years ago.

5  It _____ sunny this morning.

It _____ cloudy this morning.

6  They _____ soccer players last year.

They _____ basketball players last year.

D Read and unscramble.

1 at the party | We | not | yesterday. | were

→ We were not at the party yesterday.

2 was | last night. | She | happy | not

→ _____

3 many people | weren't | There | at the park.

→ _____

4 not | sick | was | this afternoon. | I

→ _____

5 this morning. | There | wasn't | any butter

→ _____

6 at the library | You | weren't | last Saturday.

→ _____

E Read and correct.

1 He not was at home yesterday. → He was not at home yesterday.

2 They thirsty weren't this morning. → _____

3 We wasn't at the park last night. → _____

4 It were not windy last weekend. → _____

5 You were hungry not yesterday. → _____

6 There wasn't many students. → _____

GRAMMAR POINT

Be동사 과거시제 (의문문)

- Be동사 과거시제의 의문문은 Was/Were + 주어 ...? 순으로 쓰며 '~이었니?' 또는 '~있었니?'라고 해석합니다.
- Be동사 과거시제의 의문문은 Yes/No로 대답하고, 긍정일 때는 Yes, 주어 + was/were.를 사용하고, 부정일 때는 No, 주어 + wasn't/weren't.를 사용합니다.
- 과거의 사실이나 상태를 말할 때 사용하고, yesterday, last week 등과 같은 과거 시간 부사와 함께 사용합니다.

Question	Answer	
Was I happy? (저는 행복했습니까?)	Yes, you were. (네, 그랬습니다.)	No, you weren't. (아니요, 그렇지 않았습니다.)
Were you happy? (당신은 행복했습니까?)	Yes, I was. (네, 그랬습니다.)	No, I wasn't. (아니요, 그렇지 않았습니다.)
Was he happy? (그는 행복했습니까?)	Yes, he was. (네, 그랬습니다.)	No, he wasn't. (아니요, 그렇지 않았습니다.)
Was she happy? (그녀는 행복했습니까?)	Yes, she was. (네, 그랬습니다.)	No, she wasn't. (아니요, 그렇지 않았습니다.)
Was it happy? (그것은 행복했습니까?)	Yes, it was. (네, 그랬습니다.)	No, it wasn't. (아니요, 그렇지 않았습니다.)
Were we happy? (우리는 행복했습니까?)	Yes, you were. (네, 그랬습니다.)	No, you weren't. (아니요, 그렇지 않았습니다.)
Were you happy? (당신들은 행복했습니까?)	Yes, we were. (네, 그랬습니다.)	No, we weren't. (아니요, 그렇지 않았습니다.)
Were they happy? (그들은 행복했습니까?)	Yes, they were. (네, 그랬습니다.)	No, they weren't. (아니요, 그렇지 않았습니다.)

A Read and match.

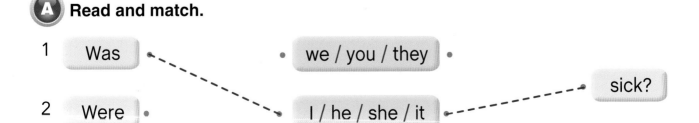

1 Was   •   • we / you / they •
                                              sick?
2 Were   •   • I / he / she / it •

B **Read and write.**

1 __Were__ they at the park last night?   Yes, they ___were___ .

2 _____ he happy yesterday?   No, he _____ .

3 _____ you at home last Monday?   Yes, I _____ .

4 _____ it foggy this morning?   No, it _____ .

5 _____ there many stars in the sky?   Yes, there _____ .

6 _____ there any cake on the dish?   No, there _____ .

C **Look and write.**

1

__Was__ he a police officer before?
__Yes__ , __he__ __was__ .

2

_____ you sad this afternoon?
_____ , _____ _____ .

3

_____ they at home yesterday?
_____ , _____ _____ .

4

_____ it windy this morning?
_____ , _____ _____ .

5

_____ you at the zoo last Sunday?
_____ , _____ _____ .

6

_____ she happy yesterday?
_____ , _____ _____ .

D Read and unscramble.

1 [you] [yesterday?] [on the playground] [Were]

→ _Were you on the playground yesterday?_

2 [sunny] [Was] [it] [this morning?]

→ _____

3 [at the zoo] [last weekend?] [Were] [they]

→ _____

4 [many students] [Were] [there] [in the classroom?]

→ _____

5 [Was] [in the bowl?] [there] [any soup]

→ _____

6 [she] [at the theater] [Was] [last night?]

→ _____

E Read and correct.

1 Were she sick last night? → _Was she sick last night?_

2 Was you at school this morning? → _____

3 Are they at the party yesterday? → _____

4 Does it rainy last weekend? → _____

5 Is your sister at work last night? → _____

6 There were many cars? → _____

Past Simple: Be Verbs (Wh- Questions)

GRAMMAR PoINT

Be동사 과거시제 (의문사가 있는 의문문)

- 의문사가 있는 be동사 과거시제의 의문문은 의문사가 맨 앞에 나와서 의문사 + was/were + 주어? 순으로 씁니다.
- 의문사 who는 사람에 대해 물을 때 사용하며 '~누구였습니까?'라고 해석합니다.
- 의문사 what은 사물에 대해 물을 때 사용하며 '~무엇이었습니까?'라고 해석합니다.
- 의문사가 있는 의문문은 Yes/No로 대답하지 않습니다.

	Question	Answer
Who	Who was he? (그는 누구였습니까?) Who was she? (그녀는 누구였습니까?) Who were they? (그들은 누구였습니까?)	He was Michael. (그는 마이클이었습니다.) She was Kelly. (그녀는 켈리였습니다.) They were John and Lisa. (그들은 존과 리사였습니다.)
What	What was it? (그것은 무엇이었습니까?) What were they? (그것들은 무엇이었습니까?)	It was a ball. (그것은 공이었습니다.) They were puppies. (그것들은 강아지들이었습니다.)

A Look, circle, and match.

1

(Who) I What   was she?

They were my parents.

2

Who I What   was it?

She was Mary.

3

Who I What   were they?

It was a mouse.

B Read and write.

1 <u>What</u> <u>were</u> they? d

2 _____ _____ he?

3 _____ _____ it?

4 _____ _____ they?

ⓐ He was Mr. Smith.   ⓑ They were my friends.
ⓒ It was a crab.   ⓓ They were bees.

C Look and write.

1

<u>Who</u> <u>was</u> he?
<u>He</u> <u>was</u> Michael.

2

_____ _____ it?
_____ _____ a rabbit.

3

_____ _____ she?
_____ _____ Kelly.

4

_____ _____ they?
_____ _____ squirrels.

5

_____ _____ they?
_____ _____ John and Lisa.

6

_____ _____ it?
_____ _____ a cat.

D Read and unscramble.

1 [were] [Who] [they?]

→ _Who were they?_ _____

2 [it?] [was] [What]

→ _____

3 [was] [she?] [Who]

→ _____

4 [What] [they?] [were]

→ _____

5 [was] [Who] [he?]

→ _____

6 [Who] [they?] [were]

→ _____

E Read and correct.

1 What was she? She was Susan. → _Who was she? She was Susan._

2 Who was it? It was a bag. → _____

3 Were who they? They were my friends. → _____

4 Was it what? It was a monkey. → _____

5 Who is he? He was Kevin. → _____

6 What are they? They were cats. → _____

A Look and write.

| was | were | wasn't | weren't |

1

He ___was___ hungry last night.

2

We _____ at the zoo yesterday.

3

You _____ at the beach.

4

I _____ tall five years ago.

5

_____ they at school last Sunday?
No, they _____.

6

_____ she sick yesterday?
Yes, she _____.

7

What _____ it?
It _____ a cat.

8

Who _____ they?
They _____ John and Lisa.

B **Read, circle, and write.**

1 We _____were_____ sleepy this afternoon.

    ⓐ is   ⓑ was   ©were

2 I _____ a doctor ten years ago.

    ⓐ am   ⓑ was   © were

3 They _____ at the museum last Sunday.

    ⓐ aren't   ⓑ wasn't   © weren't

4 She _____ sick yesterday.

    ⓐ wasn't   ⓑ isn't   © weren't

5 _____ you at home this afternoon? Yes, we _____.

    ⓐ Are, am   ⓑ Was, were   © Were, were

6 _____ it sunny this morning? No, it _____.

    ⓐ Was, wasn't   ⓑ Is, weren't   © Were, wasn't

7 _____ He was my brother.

    ⓐ Who is he?   ⓑ Who was he?   © What was it?

8 _____ They were helicopters.

    ⓐ What are they?   ⓑ Who were they?   © What were they?

9 Who were they? _____

    ⓐ Yes, they were.   ⓑ They were Carol and Jeff.   © She was Carol.

10 What was it? _____

    ⓐ It was a dog.   ⓑ It is a dog.   © No, it wasn't.

UNIT 08 Past Simple: Regular Verbs (Affirmatives)

GRAMMAR POINT

과거시제 규칙동사 (긍정문)

- 과거에 있었던 일을 말할 때 일반동사의 과거시제를 사용합니다.
- 일반동사의 과거형은 주어의 인칭과 수에 관계없이 대부분의 경우 동사 뒤에 -ed를 붙입니다.
- 일반동사의 과거형을 만드는 방법은 다음과 같습니다.
  ① 대부분의 동사 뒤에는 -ed를 붙입니다.
  ② -e로 끝나는 동사 뒤에는 -d만 붙입니다.
  ③ 자음 + y로 끝나는 동사는 y를 i로 바꾸고 -ed를 붙입니다.

Past Simple: Regular Verb			
+ -ed	play ➡ played	walk ➡ walked	visit ➡ visited
+ -d	like ➡ liked	move ➡ moved	close ➡ closed
consonant + y ➡ + -ied	cry ➡ cried	study ➡ studied	try ➡ tried

Present	Past
I / You / We / They walk. (저는 / 당신(들)은 / 우리는 / 그들은 걷습니다.) He / She / It walks. (그는 / 그녀는 / 그것은 걷습니다.)	I / You / We / They (저는 / 당신(들)은 / 우리는 / 그들은) walked yesterday. He / She / It (어제 걸었습니다.) (그는 / 그녀는 / 그것은)

A **Read and write.**

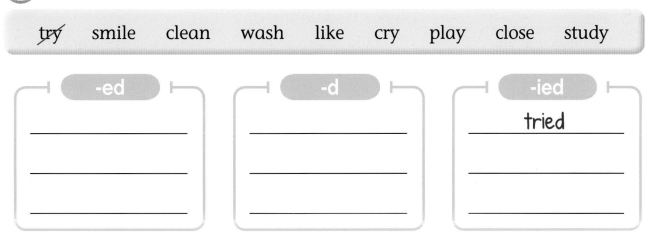

~~try~~   smile   clean   wash   like   cry   play   close   study

-ed	-d	-ied
_____	_____	tried
_____	_____	_____
_____	_____	_____

B Read and write.

Present	Past

1 We dance at the party. ➡ We ____danced____ at the party last night.

2 You walk to school. ➡ You _____ to school this morning.

3 I carry my books. ➡ I _____ my books this afternoon.

4 She moves her desk. ➡ She _____ her desk yesterday.

5 He tries the beef. ➡ He _____ the beef this afternoon.

6 It lives in the cave. ➡ It _____ in the cave last year.

C Look and write.

Sam's To-Do List for Yesterday
☑ help mother
☑ walk the dog
☑ play basketball
☑ watch a movie

Lisa and Carol's To-Do List for Yesterday
☑ clean the room
☑ study English
☑ practice tennis
☑ visit grandmother

1 Sam ____helped____ his mother yesterday.

2 He _____ his dog yesterday.

3 He _____ basketball yesterday.

4 He _____ a movie yesterday.

5 Lisa and Carol _____ their room yesterday.

6 They _____ English yesterday.

7 They _____ tennis yesterday.

8 They _____ their grandmother yesterday.

D Read and unscramble.

1 [cleaned] [yesterday.] [the house] [I]

➡ I cleaned the house yesterday.

2 [the piano] [They] [last week.] [played]

➡ _____

3 [last night.] [watched] [He] [TV]

➡ _____

4 [We] [math] [studied] [yesterday.]

➡ _____

5 [moved] [this morning.] [its wings] [It]

➡ _____

6 [at me] [She] [smiled] [this afternoon.]

➡ _____

E Read and correct.

1 She cryed last night.   ➡ She cried last night.

2 You listend to music yesterday.   ➡ _____

3 He washd his car yesterday.   ➡ _____

4 We closeed the windows last night. ➡ _____

5 They plaied baseball last week.   ➡ _____

6 I danceed on the stage last Sunday. ➡ _____

Past Simple: Irregular Verbs (Affirmatives)

GRAMMAR POINT

과거시제 불규칙동사 (긍정문)

- 과거에 있었던 일을 말할 때 일반동사의 과거시제를 사용합니다.
- 일반동사의 과거형은 주어의 인칭과 수에 관계없이 대부분의 경우 동사 뒤에 -ed를 붙입니다.
- 그러나 불규칙 동사는 과거형을 만드는데 일정한 규칙이 없습니다.

Past Simple: Irregular Verb			
have ➡ had	get ➡ got	see ➡ saw	take ➡ took
sit ➡ sat	do ➡ did	make ➡ made	go ➡ went
run ➡ ran	teach ➡ taught	come ➡ came	meet ➡ met
sing ➡ sang	ride ➡ rode	give ➡ gave	sleep ➡ slept
drink ➡ drank	write ➡ wrote	eat ➡ ate	read ➡ read

Present	Past
I / You / We / They run. (저는 / 당신(들)은 / 우리는 / 그들은 달립니다.) He / She / It runs. (그는 / 그녀는 / 그것은 달립니다.)	I / You / We / They (저는 / 당신(들)은 / 우리는 / 그들은) ran yesterday. (어제 달렸습니다.) He / She / It (그는 / 그녀는 / 그것은)

A Read and write.

Present	Past	Present	Past
do	did	make	
have		get	
take		ride	
see		sleep	
meet		sing	

B **Read and write.**

Present	Past

1 She comes to the party. ➡ She _____came_____ to the party last night.

2 You teach math. ➡ You _____ math last year.

3 He meets Tom. ➡ He _____ Tom this afternoon.

4 We sit on the sofa. ➡ We _____ on the sofa last night.

5 It drinks water. ➡ It _____ water this morning.

6 They ride bikes. ➡ They _____ bikes yesterday.

C **Look and write.**

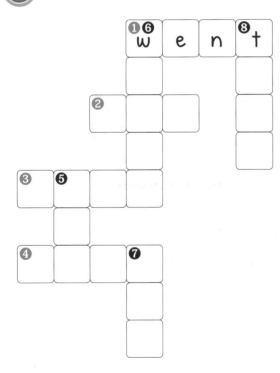

| Across ➡ |
| 1 go |
| 2 get |
| 3 make |
| 4 read |

| Down ⬇ |
| 5 eat |
| 6 write |
| 7 do |
| 8 take |

Across ➡

1 He __went__ to school yesterday.

2 I _____ up early this morning.

3 We _____ a snowman yesterday.

4 They _____ books last night.

Down ⬇

5 I _____ sandwiches this afternoon.

6 You _____ a letter last night.

7 She _____ her homework yesterday.

8 They _____ a bus this morning.

D Read and unscramble.

1 [kites] [this afternoon.] [flew] [We]

→ _We flew kites this afternoon._

2 [taught] [last year.] [He] [English]

→ _____

3 [him] [I] [saw] [yesterday.]

→ _____

4 [to school] [They] [this morning.] [ran]

→ _____

5 [You] [yesterday.] [slept] [a lot]

→ _____

6 [this morning.] [sang] [She] [a song]

→ _____

E Read and correct.

1 I haved a good time last Saturday. → _I had a good time last Saturday._

2 She doed the dishes last night. → _____

3 We goed to school yesterday. → _____

4 He writed an email last night. → _____

5 You gived presents to him. → _____

6 They eated sandwiches yesterday. → _____

Past Simple: Verbs (Negatives)

GRAMMAR POINT

과거시제 일반동사 (부정문)

● 일반동사 과거시제의 부정문은 주어 + did not(=didn't) + 동사원형 순으로 쓰고, '~하지 않았다'라고 해석합니다.
● 주어의 인칭과 수에 관계없이 did not(=didn't) 뒤에 동사원형을 씁니다.

Affirmative	Negative
I / You / We / They (저는 / 당신(들)은 / 우리는 / 그들은) went yesterday. He / She / It (그는 / 그녀는 / 그것은) (어제 갔습니다.)	I / You / We / They (저는 / 당신(들)은 / 우리는 / 그들은) didn't go yesterday. He / She / It (그는 / 그녀는 / 그것은) (어제 가지 않았습니다.)

A Look, match, and circle.

1

We   didn't take I didn't took   a taxi yesterday.
We took a bus yesterday.

2

I ⃝didn't get⃝ I didn't got   up late this morning.
I got up early this morning.

3

He   didn't clean I didn't cleans   the kitchen.
He cleaned his room.

4

She   didn't did I didn't do   the dishes.
She did her homework.

5

They   didn't lived I didn't live   in the caves.
They lived in the igloos.

B **Read and write.**

Present		Past
1 It doesn't bark.	→	It __didn't__ __bark__.
2 You don't cook spaghetti.	→	You _____ _____ spaghetti.
3 I don't play baseball.	→	I _____ _____ baseball.
4 He doesn't read a newspaper.	→	He _____ _____ a newspaper.
5 We don't have a pencil.	→	We _____ _____ a pencil.
6 They don't drink juice.	→	They _____ _____ juice.

C **Look and write.**

Nancy's To-Do List for Yesterday	Jeff and Jason's To-Do List for Yesterday
☒ get up early	☒ eat breakfast
☒ walk the dog	☒ wash hair
☒ visit grandmother	☒ study math
☒ write a diary	☒ go to the movies

1 Nancy ___didn't___ ___get___ up early yesterday.

2 She _____ _____ the dog yesterday.

3 She _____ _____ her grandmother yesterday.

4 She _____ _____ a diary yesterday.

5 Jeff and Jason _____ _____ breakfast yesterday.

6 They _____ _____ their hair yesterday.

7 They _____ _____ math yesterday.

8 They _____ _____ to the movies yesterday.

D Read and unscramble.

1 | to my house | yesterday. | They | come | didn't |

→ <u>They didn't come to my house yesterday.</u>

2 | didn't | I | last week. | my friends | meet |

→ _____

3 | dance | didn't | yesterday. | She |

→ _____

4 | We | watch | didn't | last night. | TV |

→ _____

5 | yesterday. | You | ride | didn't | a bike |

→ _____

6 | didn't | this morning. | rain | It |

→ _____

E Read and correct.

1 He didn't helped his mom last night. → <u>He didn't help his mom last night.</u>

2 We don't see a movie yesterday. → _____

3 She doesn't bake cookies last night. → _____

4 You didn't taught music last year. → _____

5 They didn't closed the door yesterday. → _____

6 He doesn't make cards last Christmas. → _____

UNIT 11

Past Simple: Verbs (Yes/No Questions)

GRAMMAR POINT

과거시제 일반동사 (의문문)

- 일반동사 과거시제의 의문문은 주어의 인칭과 수에 관계없이 Did + 주어 + 동사원형 ...? 순으로 쓰고, '~했었니?'라고 해석합니다.
- 일반동사 과거시제의 의문문은 Yes/No로 대답하고, 긍정일 때는 Yes, 주어 + did.를 사용하고, 부정일 때는 No, 주어 + didn't.를 사용합니다.

Question	Answer	
Did I / you / he / she / it drink water yesterday?	Yes, you / I / he / she / it did.	No, you / I / he / she / it didn't.
(저는 / 당신은 / 그는 / 그녀는 / 그것은 어제 물을 마셨습니까?)	(네, 그랬습니다.)	(아니요, 그러지 않았습니다.)
Did we / you / they drink water yesterday?	Yes, you / we / they did.	No, you / we / they didn't.
(우리는 / 당신들은 / 그들은 어제 물을 마셨습니까?)	(네, 그랬습니다.)	(아니요, 그러지 않았습니다.)

A Look, write, and check.

1  play

___Did___ you __play__ the piano?

✓ Yes, I did.   ☐ No, I didn't.

2 sit

_____ they _____ on the bench?

☐ Yes, they did.   ☐ No, they didn't.

3  sing

_____ he _____ a song?

☐ Yes, he did.   ☐ No, he didn't.

4  wash

_____ you _____ the car?

☐ Yes, we did.   ☐ No, we didn't.

B Read and write.

1 [do] ___Did___ he ___do___ his homework yesterday? Yes, he ___did___.

2 [live] _____ they _____ in the city? No, they _____.

3 [watch] _____ she _____ TV last night? Yes, she _____.

4 [ride] _____ you _____ a bike this afternoon? No, I _____.

5 [go] _____ they _____ to school yesterday? Yes, they _____.

6 [snow] _____ it _____ this morning? No, it _____.

C Look, follow, and write.

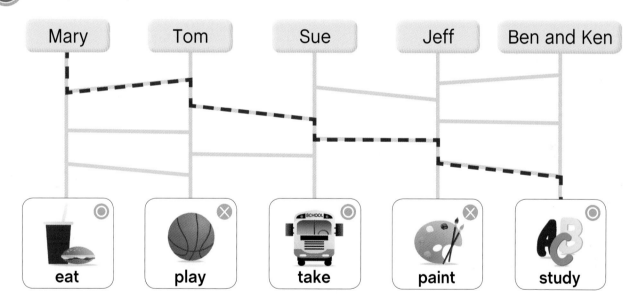

| Mary | Tom | Sue | Jeff | Ben and Ken |

eat · play · take · paint · study

1 ___Did___ Mary ___study___ English? ___Yes___, ___she___ ___did___.

2 _____ Tom _____ a school bus? _____, _____ _____.

3 _____ Sue _____ a picture? _____, _____ _____.

4 _____ Jeff _____ lunch? _____, _____ _____.

5 _____ Ben and Ken _____ basketball? _____, _____ _____.

D Read and unscramble.

1 [last night?] [it] [bark] [Did]

→ Did it bark last night?

2 [pizza] [Did] [yesterday?] [have] [you]

→ _____

3 [she] [math] [Did] [last year?] [teach]

→ _____

4 [Did] [this afternoon?] [they] [books] [read]

→ _____

5 [he] [his uncle] [visit] [last night?] [Did]

→ _____

6 [write] [Did] [a letter] [you] [yesterday?]

→ _____

E Read and correct.

1 Did they went to the zoo yesterday? → Did they go to the Zoo yesterday?

2 Did you studied English last night? → _____

3 Does he dance at the party yesterday? → _____

4 Do she cook dinner last night? → _____

5 Yes, I didn't. → _____

6 Did it rained yesterday? → _____

Past Simple: Verbs (What Questions)

GRAMMAR POINT

과거시제 일반동사 (의문사가 있는 의문문)

● 의문사 what이 있는 일반동사의 과거시제 의문문은 의문사가 맨 앞에 나와서 주어의 인칭과 수에 관계없이
  What + did + 주어 + 동사원형? 순으로 쓰고, '무엇을 ~했었니?'라고 해석합니다.
● 의문사가 있는 의문문은 Yes/No로 대답하지 않습니다.

Question	Answer
What did I you he she it do yesterday? (저는 / 당신은 / 그는 / 그녀는 / 그것은 어제 무엇을 했습니까?)	You washed your dog yesterday. (당신은 어제 당신의 개를 목욕시켰습니다.) I did my homework yesterday. (저는 어제 숙제를 하였습니다.) He studied math yesterday. (그는 어제 수학을 공부하였습니다.) She went to the park yesterday. (그녀는 어제 공원에 갔습니다.) It chased a butterfly yesterday. (그것은 어제 나비를 쫓았습니다.)
What did we you they do yesterday? (우리는 / 당신들은 / 그들은 어제 무엇을 했습니까?)	You rode horses yesterday. (당신들은 어제 말을 탔습니다.) We played soccer yesterday. (우리는 어제 축구를 하였습니다.) They flew kites yesterday. (그들은 어제 연을 날렸습니다.)

A Read and match.

1 What did you do yesterday?   •   He exercised yesterday.

2 What did he do yesterday?   •   It slept a lot yesterday.

3 What did it do yesterday?   •   I rode a bike yesterday.

B Read and write.

1 <u>What</u> <u>did</u> they <u>do</u> last night?　　　**b**

2 _____ _____ you _____ yesterday?　　___

3 _____ _____ he _____ last weekend?　　___

4 _____ _____ she _____ this morning?　　___

ⓐ She studied English this morning.

ⓑ They wrote a letter last night.

ⓒ I visited my grandparents yesterday.

ⓓ He made an airplane last weekend.

C Look and write.

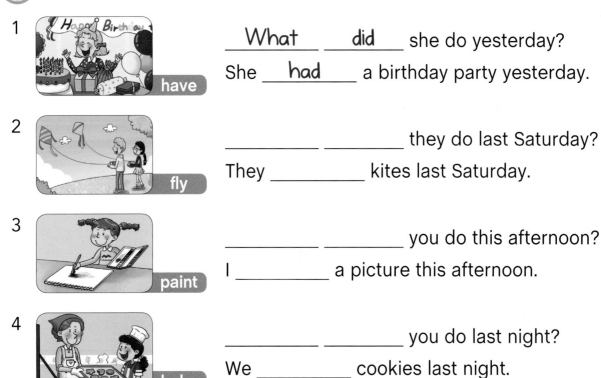

1 have

<u>What</u> <u>did</u> she do yesterday?

She <u>had</u> a birthday party yesterday.

2 fly

_____ _____ they do last Saturday?

They _____ kites last Saturday.

3 paint

_____ _____ you do this afternoon?

I _____ a picture this afternoon.

4 bake

_____ _____ you do last night?

We _____ cookies last night.

5 go

_____ _____ he do yesterday?

He _____ to school yesterday.

D Read and unscramble.

1 [you] [What] [do] [last weekend?] [did]

→ What did you do last weekend?

2 [last night?] [did] [he] [do] [What]

→ _____

3 [did] [you] [What] [yesterday?] [do]

→ _____

4 [do] [this morning?] [did] [What] [it]

→ _____

5 [What] [they] [did] [last week?] [do]

→ _____

6 [do] [What] [this afternoon?] [did] [she]

→ _____

E Read and correct.

1 What does he do yesterday?   He went to the hospital yesterday.

→ What did he do yesterday?

2 What did you do last Sunday?   I clean my room last Sunday.

→ _____

3 What did it does this morning?   It ate fish this morning.

→ _____

4 What did she do last night?   She does her homework last night.

→ _____

5 What did they did yesterday?   They played soccer yesterday.

→ _____

A **Read and write.**

1 `close`   You ___closed___ the window last night.

2 `walk`   They _____ in the park yesterday.

3 `carry`   I _____ my toys last weekend.

4 `sit`   We _____ on the bench this afternoon.

5 `get`   She _____ up early this morning.

6 `fly`   You _____ a kite last Saturday.

B **Look and write.**

| meet | visit | ~~ride~~ | paint |

1

He ___didn't___ ___ride___ a bike yesterday.

He ___rode___ a horse yesterday.

2

She _____ _____ her aunt last weekend.

She _____ her grandmother last weekend.

3

I _____ _____ the wall last night.

I _____ a picture last night.

4

They _____ _____ Kelly this afternoon.

They _____ Brian this afternoon.

C Read and write.

Affirmative		Question
1 She played the piano.	➡	__Did__ she __play__ the piano?
2 They studied English.	➡	_____ they _____ English?
3 You danced at the party.	➡	_____ you _____ at the party?
4 He wrote a diary.	➡	_____ he _____ a diary?
5 It drank water last night.	➡	_____ it _____ water last night?
6 They came home.	➡	_____ they _____ home?

D Read, circle, and write.

1 What _____did_____ you do yesterday?

    ⓐ do   ⓑ did   ⓒ does

2 What did he _____ last weekend?

    ⓐ do   ⓑ does   ⓒ did

3 What _____ they _____ last Saturday?

    ⓐ does, do   ⓑ did, does   ⓒ did, do

4 What did she do last night? She _____ soup last night.

    ⓐ cooks   ⓑ cooked   ⓒ is cooking

5 What did it do this morning? It _____ fish this morning.

    ⓐ ate   ⓑ eats   ⓒ is eating

6 What did you do last night? I _____ a shower last night.

    ⓐ take   ⓑ taked   ⓒ took

Future: Will (Affirmatives, Negatives)

GRAMMAR POINT

미래시제 Will (긍정문과 부정문)

- will은 미래에 일어날 일에 대해 말할 때 사용합니다.
- 미래시제 will의 긍정문은 주어의 인칭과 수에 관계없이 주어 + will + 동사원형 순으로 쓰고, '~ 할 것이다'라고 해석합니다.
- 미래시제 will의 부정문은 will 다음에 not을 붙여서 주어 + will not(=won't) + 동사원형 순으로 쓰고, '~하지 않을 것이다'라고 해석합니다.
- 미래시제 will은 tomorrow, next week, next year 등과 같은 미래 시간 부사와 함께 사용합니다.

Affirmative	Negative
I / You / We / They He / She / It **will be happy.**	I / You / We / They He / She / It **won't be happy.**
(저는 / 당신(들)은 / 우리는 / 그들은 / 그는 / 그녀는 / 그것은 / 행복할 것입니다.)	(저는 / 당신(들)은 / 우리는 / 그들은 / 그는 / 그녀는 / 그것은 / 행복하지 않을 것입니다.)
I / You / We / They He / She / It **will come.**	I / You / We / They He / She / It **won't come.**
(저는 / 당신(들)은 / 우리는 / 그들은 / 그는 / 그녀는 / 그것은 / 올 것입니다.)	(저는 / 당신(들)은 / 우리는 / 그들은/ 그는 / 그녀는 / 그것은 / 오지 않을 것입니다.)

* won't = will not

Past — yesterday   Present — now   Future — tomorrow

A Read and circle.

1 I will am I (will be) a scientist.

2 He will watch I will watches TV.

3 She won't be I won't is happy.

4 We won't went I won't go zoo.

5 You will are I will be at school.

6 She will eat I will eats dinner tonight.

7 It won't be I won't was rainy.

8 They won't took I won't take a bus.

B **Read and write.**

Present	Future

1 It is cloudy. → It ___will___ ___be___ cloudy tomorrow.

2 They are not teachers. → They _____ _____ teachers next year.

3 I write a letter. → I _____ _____ a letter tonight.

4 You don't play the piano. → You _____ _____ the piano tomorrow.

5 He walks to school. → He _____ _____ to school next week.

6 We don't clean the house. → We _____ _____ the house tomorrow.

C **Look and write.**

1

He ___will___ ___study___ English.

He ___won't___ ___study___ science.

2

I _____ _____ a doctor.

I _____ _____ a nurse.

3

They _____ _____ a bus.

They _____ _____ a taxi.

4

She _____ _____ cake.

She _____ _____ ice cream.

5

We _____ _____ at home.

We _____ _____ outside.

D **Read and unscramble.**

1 | will | | a bike | | She | | next weekend. | | ride |

→ She will ride a bike next weekend.

2 | go | | We | | tomorrow. | | will | | fishing |

→ _____

3 | be | | You | | will | | in the future. | | a singer |

→ _____

4 | won't | | next Sunday. | | soccer | | He | | play |

→ _____

5 | tomorrow. | | be | | won't | | snowy | | It |

→ _____

6 | They | | a movie | | watch | | tonight. | | won't |

→ _____

E **Read and correct.**

1   It will is sunny tomorrow.   → It will be sunny tomorrow.

2   He be will at home this Sunday.   → _____

3   I buy will a computer tomorrow.   → _____

4   She won't listens to the radio tonight. → _____

5   You will went on a picnic next week. → _____

6   They walk won't the dog tomorrow.   → _____

GRAMMAR POINT

미래시제 Will (의문문)

- 미래시제 will의 의문문은 주어의 인칭과 수에 관계없이 문장의 맨 앞에 will을 붙여 Will + 주어 + 동사원형 ...? 순으로 쓰며 '~ 할 것입니까?'라고 해석합니다.
- 미래시제 will의 의문문은 Yes/No로 대답하며, 긍정일 때는 Yes, 주어 + will.를 사용하고, 부정일 때는 No, 주어 + won't.를 사용합니다.
- 의문사 what이 있는 의문문은 의문사가 맨 앞에 나와서 What + will + 주어 + 동사원형 ...? 순으로 쓰고 Yes/No로 대답하지 않습니다.

Question			Answer				
Will	I you he she it	be happy? go to the park?	Yes,	you I he she it	will.	No,	you I he she it	won't.
(저는 / 당신은 / 그는 / 그녀는 / 그것은 행복할 것입니까?/ 공원에 갈 것입니까?)			(네, 그럴 것입니다.)			(아니요, 그러지 않을 것입니다.)	
Will	we you they	be happy? go to the park?	Yes,	you we they	will.	No,	you we they	won't.
(우리는 / 당신들은 / 그들은 행복할 것입니까? / 공원에 갈 것입니까?)			(네, 그럴 것입니다.)			(아니요, 그러지 않을 것입니다.)	
What will you be in the future? (당신은 미래에 무엇이 될 것입니까?) What will you do tomorrow? (당신은 내일 무엇을 할 것입니까?)			I will be a doctor in the future. (저는 미래에 의사가 될 것입니다.) I will go to the beach tomorrow. (저는 내일 바닷가에 갈 것입니다.)				

A Read, write, and check.

1 ___Will___ you be at home tomorrow? ☐ Yes, I am. ☑ No, I won't.

2 _____ it be cold next week? ☐ Yes, it will. ☐ No, it isn't.

3 _____ he play baseball next Sunday? ☐ Yes, he will. ☐ No, he isn't.

4 _____ they go hiking tomorrow? ☐ Yes, they are. ☐ No, they won't.

B Look and write.

1
play

___Will___ they ___play___ baseball?

___Yes___ , ___they___ ___will___ .

2
be

_____ it _____ sunny?

_____ , _____ _____ .

3
help

_____ he _____ the old woman?

_____ , _____ _____ .

4
buy

_____ _____ she do?

_____ _____ _____ ice cream.

5
be

_____ _____ you be?

_____ _____ _____ a police officer.

C Read and write.

1 ___What___ ___will___ she do tomorrow? | c |

2 _____ _____ they do this Sunday? | |

3 _____ _____ he be in the future? | |

4 _____ _____ you be in the future? | |

ⓐ They will go to the zoo this Sunday. ⓑ I will be a pianist in the future.

ⓒ She will go to school tomorrow.   ⓓ He will be a doctor in the future.

50

D **Read and unscramble.**

1 [he] [math] [tomorrow?] [Will] [study]

→ _Will he study math tomorrow?_

2 [next weekend?] [visit] [you] [your uncle] [Will]

→ _____

3 [be] [she] [in the future?] [Will] [a cook]

→ _____

4 [you] [Will] [be] [hungry?]

→ _____

5 [will] [do] [What] [next Sunday?] [they]

→ _____

6 [be] [will] [in the future?] [What] [he]

→ _____

E **Read and correct.**

1 Will you did your homework? → _Will you do your homework?_

2 Will they are teachers next year? → _____

3 Will she makes sandwiches? → _____

4 Will be he busy next Monday? → _____

5 What will she does next weekend? → _____

6 Will what you be in the future? → _____

Future: Be Going to (Affirmatives, Negatives)

UNIT 15

GRAMMAR POINT

미래시제 Be Going to (긍정문과 부정문)

- 미래시제 be going to 구문은 미리 예정된 일이나 미래의 계획을 말할 때 사용합니다.
- 미래시제 be going to 구문의 긍정문은 주어 + be동사 + going to + 동사원형 순으로 쓰며, '~할 예정이다' 또는 '~할 것이다'라고 해석합니다.
- 미래시제 be going to 구문의 부정문은 be동사 다음에 not을 붙여서 주어 + be동사 + not + going to + 동사원형 순으로 쓰고, '~하지 않을 예정이다' 또는 '~하지 않을 것이다'라고 해석합니다.

Affirmative			Negative		
I	am going to	be sad. walk.	I	am not going to	be sad. walk.
He / She / It	is going to		He / She / It	is not going to	
We / You / They	are going to		We / You / They	are not going to	
(저는 / 그는 / 그녀는 / 그것은 / 우리는 / 당신(들)은 / 그들은 슬플 것입니다. / 걸을 예정입니다.)			(저는 / 그는 / 그녀는 / 그것은 / 우리는 / 당신(들)은 / 그들은 슬프지 않을 것입니다. / 걷지 않을 예정입니다.)		

Past	Present	Future
yesterday	now	tomorrow

A Read and circle.

1 She ((is going to watch)I is going to watches) a movie tonight.

2 We (am going to play I are going to play) outside tomorrow.

3 I (am going to buy I are going to buy) a bike tomorrow.

4 He (isn't going to is I isn't going to be) late for school next week.

5 You (aren't going to walk I aren't going to walked) the dog next weekend.

6 She (isn't going to does I isn't going to do) the dishes tonight.

B Read, match, and write.

1 I am hungry.

2 He is in the bakery.

3 They have a cold.

4 She gets up late.

5 You don't like math.

They _____ _____ a doctor.
see

I __am going to__ __eat__ pizza.
eat

You _____ _____ math.
study

He _____ _____ bread.
buy

She _____ _____ on time.
be

C Look and write.

1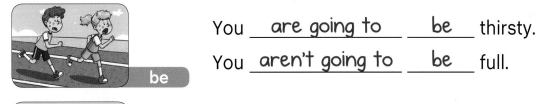
be

You __are going to__ __be__ thirsty.
You __aren't going to__ __be__ full.

2 **visit**

He _____ _____ America.
He _____ _____ China.

3 **have**

They _____ _____ a party.
They _____ _____ a class.

4 **buy**

She _____ _____ bread.
She _____ _____ toys.

D Read and unscramble.

1 (cook) (They) (tonight.) (are going to) (spaghetti)

→ _They are going to cook spaghetti tonight._

2 (isn't going to) (the violin) (She) (play) (next Monday.)

→ _____

3 (He) (next weekend.) (wash) (is going to) (the car)

→ _____

4 (take) (aren't going to) (a train) (tomorrow.) (We)

→ _____

5 (tonight.) (watch) (I) (TV) (am going to)

→ _____

6 (be) (at home) (are going to) (You) (next week.)

→ _____

E Read and correct.

1 He is going to studies English.   → _He is going to study English._

2 We are going to going to the park.   → _____

3 I am going to meeting my friend.   → _____

4 They not are going to drink coffee.   → _____

5 She is going to not go to a concert.   → _____

6 It is not going to eats bananas.   → _____

UNIT 16 Future: Be Going to (Yes/No Questions, What Questions)

GRAMMAR POINT

미래시제 Be Going to (의문문)

- 미래시제 be going to 구문의 의문문은 be동사 + 주어 + going to + 동사원형 ...? 순으로 쓰고, '~할 예정입니까?' 또는 '~할 것입니까?'라고 해석합니다.
- 미래시제 be going to 구문의 의문문은 Yes/No로 대답하며, 긍정일 때는 Yes, 주어 + be 동사.를 사용하고, 부정일 때는 No, 주어 + be동사 + not.를 사용합니다.
- 의문사 what이 있는 의문문은 의문사가 맨 앞에 나와서 What + will + 주어 + 동사 ...? 순으로 쓰고, Yes/No로 대답하지 않습니다.

Question	Answer	
Am I Are you Is he going to be happy? Is she going to come? Is it (저는 / 당신은 / 그는 / 그녀는 / 그것은 행복할 것입니까? / 올 예정입니까?)	Yes, you are. Yes, I am. Yes, he is. Yes, she is. Yes, it is. (네, 그럴 것입니다.)	No, you aren't. No, I'm not. No, he isn't. No, she isn't. No, it isn't. (아니요, 그렇지 않을 것입니다.)
Are we going to be happy? Are you going to come? Are they (우리는 / 당신들은 / 그들은 행복할 것입니까? / 올 예정입니까?)	Yes, you are. Yes, we are. Yes, they are. (네, 그럴 것입니다.)	No, you aren't. No, we aren't. No, they aren't. (아니요, 그렇지 않을 것입니다.)
What are you going to be in the future? (당신은 미래에 무엇이 될 것입니까?) What are you going to do next week? (당신은 다음 주에 무엇을 할 예정입니까?)	I am going to be a doctor in the future. (저는 미래에 의사가 될 것입니다.) I am going to visit Paris next week. (저는 다음 주에 파리를 방문할 예정입니다.)	

A Read and match.

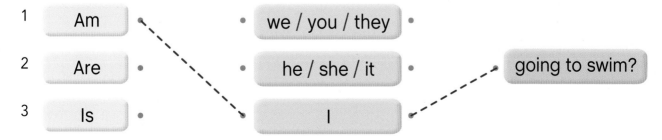

1 Am   ·   · we / you / they ·

2 Are   ·   · he / she / it   ·   going to swim?

3 Is   ·   · I   ·

B **Read and write.**

1 __Are__ they __going to__ swim?   Yes, ____they____ ____are____ .

2 _____ it _____ rain?   No, _____ _____ .

3 _____ he _____ study?   Yes, _____ _____ .

4 _____ you _____ cook?   No, _____ _____ .

5 _____ she _____ be at home?   Yes, _____ _____ .

6 _____ you _____ eat pizza?   No, _____ _____ .

C **Look and write.**

1   **be**   ____Is____ she ____going to____ ____be____ happy?

____No____ , ____she____ ____isn't____ .

2   **sleep**   _____ they _____ _____ at home?

_____ , _____ _____ .

3   **wear**   _____ you _____ _____ a coat?

_____ , _____ _____ .

4   **brush**   _____ they _____ _____ the dog?

_____ , _____ _____ .

5   **watch**   _____ _____ she _____ do?

_____ _____ _____ TV.

6   **be**   _____ _____ you _____ be?

_____ _____ _____ a doctor.

D **Read and unscramble.**

1 | to the hospital? | Are | going to | you | go |

→ _Are you going to go to the hospital?_

2 | he | play | Is | computer games? | going to |

→ _____

3 | going to | Are | water? | they | drink |

→ _____

4 | read | she | going to | Is | a book? |

→ _____

5 | be? | What | going to | is | he |

→ _____

6 | are | you | do? | What | going to |

→ _____

E **Read and correct.**

1 Is he going to stays at home?   → _Is he going to stay at home?_

2 Are we going to playing soccer?   → _____

3 Are what they going to be?   → _____

4 What is she going to does?   → _____

5 Are you clean going to your room? → _____

6 Is she going to takes a taxi?   → _____

A **Read and write.**

Present	Future
1 They are hungry.	→ They ___will___ ___be___ hungry soon.
2 He isn't at school.	→ He _____ _____ at school tomorrow.
3 She is a doctor.	→ She _____ _____ a doctor next year.
4 You don't ride on a boat.	→ You _____ _____ on a boat tomorrow.
5 It rains.	→ It _____ _____ next week.
6 I don't eat ice cream.	→ I _____ _____ ice cream tonight.

B **Look and write.**

do	~~study~~	be	play

1 ___Will___ ___he___ ___study___ English?

Yes, he will.

2 _____ _____ _____ soccer?

No, they won't.

3 _____ _____ _____?

She will eat dessert.

4 _____ _____ _____?

I will be a scientist.

C Look and write.

Affirmative	Negative
1 She is going to buy a car.	She isn't going to buy a car.
2	We aren't going to do our homework.
3 I am going to walk the dog.	
4	He isn't going to sleep.
5 They are going to go shopping.	
6	It isn't going to be sunny.

D Read, circle, and write.

1 _____Are_____ you going to _____ride_____ a horse?

  ⓐ Are, ride   ⓑ Is, rides   ⓒ Am, ride

2 _____ he _____ take a bus tomorrow?

  ⓐ Is, goes to   ⓑ Is, going to   ⓒ Are, go to

3 _____ they going to _____ TV?

  ⓐ Are, watches   ⓑ Am, watching   ⓒ Are, watch

4 _____ she going to _____ a singer?

  ⓐ Is, be   ⓑ Are, be   ⓒ Is, am

5 Are you going to wash the car? _____

  ⓐ Yes, it is.   ⓑ No, I'm not.   ⓒ Yes, they are.

6 _____ She is going to swim.

  ⓐ What will she be?   ⓑ What is she going to be?   ⓒ What is she going to do?

Adverbs of Manner

GRAMMAR POINT

양태부사

- 양태부사는 주로 동사의 뒤쪽에 위치하여 동사의 의미를 더해주고 수식해 주는 역할을 합니다.
- 양태부사는 어떤 일이 어떻게 일어났는지 나타내며 '~하게'로 해석합니다.
- 양태부사를 만드는 방법은 다음과 같습니다.
  ① 대부분의 형용사 뒤에 -ly를 붙입니다.
  ② -y로 끝나는 형용사는 y를 i로 바꾸고 -ly를 붙입니다.
- 일정한 규칙 없이 불규칙적으로 변하는 부사도 있습니다.

Regular Adverb		Irregular Adverb	
+ -ly	**-y ➡ + -ily**		
slow (느린) ➡ slowly (느리게)	easy (쉬운) ➡ easily (쉽게)	good (좋은) ➡ well (잘)	
quiet (조용한) ➡ quietly (조용하게)	happy (행복한) ➡ happily (행복하게)	late (늦은) ➡ late (늦게)	
careful (조심스러운) ➡ carefully (조심스럽게)	angry (화가 난) ➡ angrily (화가 나서)	fast (빠른) ➡ fast (빠르게)	
loud (소리가 큰) ➡ loudly (크게)	heavy (무거운) ➡ heavily (무겁게)	early (이른) ➡ early (일찍)	

A Read and write.

Adjective	Adverb	Adjective	Adverb
bad	badly	good	
heavy		loud	
fast		easy	
quiet		beautiful	

B Read and write.

1 | hard | She works. ➡ <u>She works hard.</u>

2 | early | You come. ➡ _____

3 | angry | He says. ➡ _____

4 | quiet | They talk. ➡ _____

5 | happy | I smile. ➡ _____

6 | late | We get up ➡ _____

C Read and write.

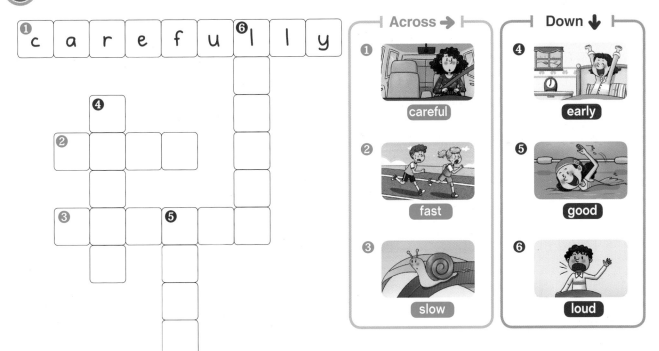

Across ➡
① careful
② fast
③ slow

Down ⬇
④ early
⑤ good
⑥ loud

Across ➡

1 I drive <u>carefully</u>.

2 We run _____.

3 It moves _____.

Down ⬇

4 She gets up _____.

5 You swim _____.

6 He speaks _____.

D **Read and unscramble.**

1 [beautifully.] [You] [dance]

➡ _You dance beautifully._

2 [his homework] [He] [quickly.] [finishes]

➡ _____

3 [noisily.] [bark] [They]

➡ _____

4 [the violin] [play] [well.] [I]

➡ _____

5 [cries] [She] [sadly.]

➡ _____

6 [hard.] [study] [We] [English]

➡ _____

E **Read and correct.**

1 He rides carefully a horse. ➡ _He rides a horse carefully._

2 She solves the problem easy. ➡ _____

3 You write a letter neat. ➡ _____

4 We happily live. ➡ _____

5 I drive a car fastly. ➡ _____

6 They go to bed lately. ➡ _____

Adverbs of Frequency I

GRAMMAR POINT

빈도부사 I

- 빈도부사는 어떤 일을 얼마나 자주하는지 나타내는 부사입니다.
- 반복적으로 일어나는 일과 습관적인 것을 말할 때 사용합니다.
- 빈도부사는 빈도에 따라 always 〉 usually 〉 often 〉 sometimes 〉 never가 있습니다.
- 빈도부사는 be동사 뒤, 일반동사 앞에 위치합니다.

Adverb of Frequency + Verb	Be Verb + Adverb of Frequency
I always get up early. (저는 항상 일찍 일어납니다.) You often get up early. (당신은 자주 일찍 일어납니다.) He never gets up early. (그는 결코 일찍 일어나지 않습니다.)	I am always late. (저는 항상 늦습니다.) You are often late (당신은 자주 늦습니다.) He is never late. (그는 결코 늦지 않습니다.)

Question	Answer
How often do you study English? (당신은 얼마나 자주 영어를 공부합니까?) How often does he play soccer? (그는 얼마나 자주 축구를 합니까?) How often are you angry? (당신은 얼마나 자주 화가 납니까?)	I usually study English. (저는 보통 영어를 공부합니다.) He often plays soccer. (그는 자주 축구를 합니다.) I am sometimes angry. (저는 종종 화가 납니다.)

A Read, write, and circle.

Percentage	Adverb of Frequency		Sentence
100%	1	always	They ⓐ are ⓑ tired at night.
90%	2		He ⓐ listens ⓑ to music.
70%	3		I ⓐ am ⓑ busy.
50%	4		She ⓐ eats ⓑ cookies.
0%	5		You ⓐ go ⓑ to the concert.

B **Read and write.**

1 | sometimes / watch | I <u>sometimes</u> <u>watch</u> a movie.

2 | never / be | She _____ _____ angry.

3 | usually / be | You _____ _____ at home.

4 | often / take | They _____ _____ a subway.

5 | always / walk | He _____ _____ to school.

6 | sometimes / bark | It _____ _____ .

C **Look, follow, and write.**

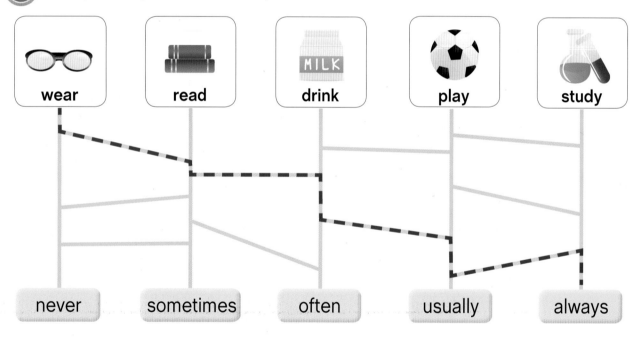

wear   read   drink   play   study

never   sometimes   often   usually   always

1 How often do you wear glasses? I <u>always</u> <u>wear</u> glasses.

2 How often do you read books? I _____ _____ books.

3 How often do you drink milk? I _____ _____ milk.

4 How often do you play soccer? I _____ _____ soccer.

5 How often do you study science? I _____ _____ science.

D Read and unscramble.

1 [always] [his homework.] [He] [does]

   → _He always does his homework._

2 [get up] [We] [early.] [usually]

   → _____

3 [You] [play] [never] [the guitar.]

   → _____

4 [sometimes] [She] [the dishes.] [washes]

   → _____

5 [sleepy.] [often] [am] [I]

   → _____

6 [always] [It] [sunny.] [is]

   → _____

E Read and correct.

1 You usually are at school.   → _You are usually at school._

2 I write often a diary.   → _____

3 He is late sometimes.   → _____

4 They bake cookies never.   → _____

5 She exercises often.   → _____

6 We do our homework always. → _____

Adverbs of Frequency Ⅱ

GRAMMAR PoInT

빈도부사 Ⅱ

- 빈도부사는 어떤 일을 얼마나 자주하는지 나타내는 부사입니다.
- 반복적으로 일어나는 일과 습관적인 것을 말할 때 사용합니다.
- 얼마나 자주 하는지 구체적인 횟수를 들어 나타낼 수 있습니다.
  ① every 뒤에 day / week / month / year 등의 구체적인 기간을 붙여서 나타내기도 합니다.
  ② 구체적인 횟수 once, twice, three times, ⋯ times와 뒤에 기간을 나타내는 a day / a week / a month / a year 등을 사용해서 얼마 동안에 몇 번 하는지 더 구체적으로 표현할 수도 있습니다.

Question	Answer
How often do you take a shower? (당신은 얼마나 자주 샤워를 합니까?)	I take a shower every day. (저는 매일 샤워를 합니다.)
How often does she do the laundry? (그녀는 얼마나 자주 세탁을 합니까?)	She does the laundry once a week. (그녀는 일주일에 한 번 세탁을 합니다.)
How often does he go to the movies? (그는 얼마나 자주 영화 보러 갑니까?)	He goes to the movies twice a month. (그는 한 달에 두 번 영화 보러 갑니다.)
How often do they brush their teeth? (그들은 얼마나 자주 이를 닦습니까?)	They brush their teeth three times a day. (그들은 하루에 세 번 이를 닦습니다.)

A Read and circle.

1 She cleans the house (three times a week) I a week three times .

2 We play basketball week every I every week .

3 He washes the car a month twice I twice a month .

4 I visit the museum every month I every months .

5 You eat spaghetti once a week I a week once .

6 They have a Christmas party every years I every year .

B Read and write.

1 [2 / month]   I write a letter _____twice_____ _____a month_____ .

2 [3 / day]   We brush our teeth _____ _____ .

3 [every day]   He checks his email _____ _____ .

4 [1 / week]   You listen to the radio _____ _____ .

5 [every week]   She does the laundry _____ _____ .

6 [2 / year]   They go on a picnic _____ _____ .

C Read and write.

Tom's Weekly Schedule							
	Mon	Tue	Wed	Thu	Fri	Sat	Sun
have breakfast	O	O	O	O	O	O	O
walk the dog	X	X	X	X	X	O	X
watch TV	X	X	O	X	X	O	X
speak English	O	O	O	O	O	O	O
go hiking	X	X	X	X	X	X	O
ride a bike	X	O	X	O	X	O	X

1 How often does Tom have breakfast? He has breakfast _____every_____ _____day_____ .

2 How often does he walk the dog?   He walks the dog _____ _____ .

3 How often does he watch TV?   He watches TV _____ _____ .

4 How often does he speak English?   He speaks English _____ _____ .

5 How often does he go hiking?   He goes hiking _____ _____ .

6 How often does he ride a bike?   He rides a bike _____ _____ .

D Read and unscramble.

1 [to the library] [We] [a week.] [go] [once]

→ We go to the library once a week.

2 [take] [a week.] [a bus] [They] [three times]

→ _____

3 [She] [every] [day.] [juice] [drinks]

→ _____

4 [a car] [I] [twice] [drive] [a month.]

→ _____

5 [his mother] [a week.] [helps] [once] [He]

→ _____

6 [meet] [weekend.] [You] [every] [your friend]

→ _____

E Read and correct.

1 They brush the dog every weeks. → They brush the dog every week.

2 You swim twice weeks. → _____

3 He reads a newspaper day every. → _____

4 She stays at home every days. → _____

5 We eat steak a week once. → _____

6 I cook dinner three times weeks. → _____

Units 17-19

A Look and write.

1

noisy

It is a ___noisy___ bird.
It sings ___noisily___.

2

good

She is a _____ singer.
She sings _____.

3

loud

He is a _____ speaker.
He speaks _____.

4

fast

I am a _____ runner.
I run _____.

B Read and write.

Percentage	Adverb of Frequency	Verb	Sentence
0%	1 never	eat	You ___never___ ___eat___ cookies.
70%	2	speak	He _____ _____ English.
100%	3	go	We _____ _____ to the park.
90%	4	write	She _____ _____ a letter.
70%	5	be	They _____ _____ late.
50%	6	be	It _____ _____ cold.
90%	7	be	I _____ _____ happy.

C Read and write.

1 How often do you take a subway?

1 / week   I take a subway ____once____ ____a week____.

2 How often do you eat meals?

3 / day   We eat meals _____ _____.

3 How often do you wash your hair?

every day   I wash my hair _____ _____.

4 How often does he study English?

2 / week   He studies English _____ _____.

5 How often do they have a Halloween party?

every year   They have a Halloween party _____ _____.

6 How often does she visit America?

2 / year   She visits America _____ _____.

D Read, circle, and write.

1 She studies English ____hard____.

   ⓐ hard   ⓑ easy   ⓒ hardly

2 We get up _____.

   ⓐ earlily   ⓑ lately   ⓒ early

3 They _____ _____ sleepy in class.

   ⓐ never are   ⓑ are never   ⓒ never do

4 He _____ _____ computer games.

   ⓐ play often   ⓑ often plays   ⓒ plays often

5 I see a doctor _____ _____.

   ⓐ every year   ⓑ year every   ⓒ every years

6 You clean the classroom _____ _____.

   ⓐ a week three times   ⓑ three times a week   ⓒ three times weeks

What / What Color

GRAMMAR POINT

의문사 What

- 의문사 what은 사물에 관한 것을 물을 때 사용하고, '무엇'이라고 해석합니다.
- be동사와 함께 쓰일 경우 What + be동사 + 주어? 순으로 씁니다.
- 일반 동사와 함께 쓰일 경우 What + do/does + 주어 + 동사원형? 순으로 씁니다.
- 의문사 what이 명사와 결합하여 쓰일 경우 '무슨'이라고 해석합니다.
- 의문사 what이 명사와 결합하여 be동사와 함께 쓰일 경우 What + 명사 + be동사 + 주어? 순으로 씁니다.
- 의문사 what이 명사와 결합하여 일반동시와 함께 쓰일 경우 What + 명사 + do/does + 주어 + 동사원형? 순으로 씁니다.

What ...?	What + Noun ...?
What is it? It is a dog. (그것은 무엇입니까? 그것은 개입니다.)	What color is it? It is brown. (그것은 무슨 색입니까? 그것은 갈색입니다.)
What are they? They are dogs. (그것들은 무엇입니까? 그것들은 개입니다.)	What color are they? They are brown. (그것들은 무슨 색입니까? 그것들은 갈색입니다.)
What do you like? I like dolls. (당신은 무엇을 좋아합니까? 저는 인형을 좋아합니다.)	What color do you like? I like orange. (당신은 무슨 색을 좋아합니까? 저는 오렌지색을 좋아합니다.)
What does she like? She likes dolls. (그녀는 무엇을 좋아합니까? 그녀는 인형을 좋아합니다.)	What color does she like? She likes orange. (그녀는 무슨 색을 좋아합니까? 그녀는 오렌지색을 좋아합니다.)

A Read and match.

1 What is it?   •   • I like yellow.

2 What color are they?   •   • It is a computer.

3 What does she have?   •   • She has gloves.

4 What color do you like? •   • They are green.

B Read and write.

1 <u>What</u> <u>are</u> <u>they</u> ? They are socks.

2 _____ _____ _____ ? It is an apple.

3 _____ _____ _____ _____ ? They are black.

4 _____ _____ _____ _____ ? I like flowers.

5 _____ _____ _____ _____ _____ ? He likes blue.

6 _____ _____ _____ _____ ? We have books.

C Look and write.

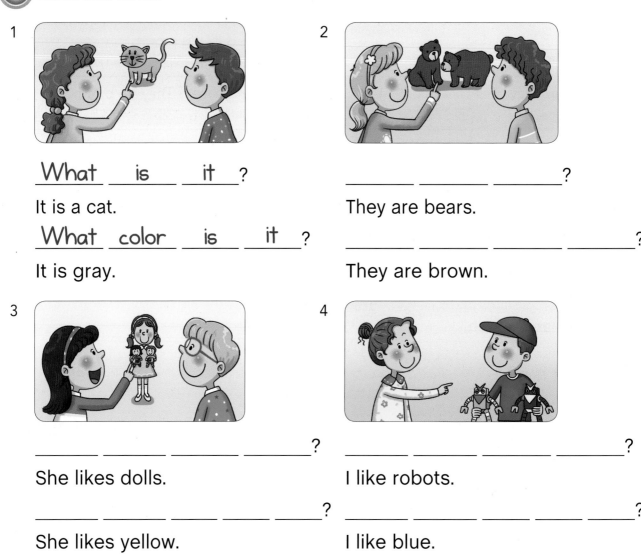

1
<u>What</u> <u>is</u> <u>it</u> ?
It is a cat.
<u>What</u> <u>color</u> <u>is</u> <u>it</u> ?
It is gray.

2
_____ _____ _____ ?
They are bears.
_____ _____ _____ _____ ?
They are brown.

3
_____ _____ _____ _____ ?
She likes dolls.
_____ _____ _____ _____ _____ ?
She likes yellow.

4
_____ _____ _____ _____ ?
I like robots.
_____ _____ _____ _____ _____ ?
I like blue.

D Read and unscramble.

1 | like? | | she | | What | | does |

→ ___What does she like?___

2 | color | | they? | | are | | What |

→ _____

3 | is | | What | | it? |

→ _____

4 | What | | do | | have? | | you |

→ _____

5 | he | | sport | | What | | does | | like? |

→ _____

6 | is | | What | | it? | | color |

→ _____

E Read and correct.

1 Are what they? → ___What are they?___

2 Color what is it? → _____

3 Does what she have? → _____

4 What animal you do like? → _____

5 What they are? → _____

6 Does what color he like? → _____

Who / Whose

GRAMMAR PoINT

의문사 Who
- 의문사 who는 사람에 관해 물을 때 사용하고, '누구'라고 해석합니다.
- be동사와 함께 쓰일 경우 Who + be동사 + 주어? 순으로 씁니다.

의문사 Whose
- 의문사 whose는 물건의 소유를 물을 때 사용하고, '누구의'라고 해석합니다.
- be동사와 함께 쓰일 경우 의문사 Whose + 명사 + be동사 + 주어? 순으로 씁니다.

Who ...?	Whose + Noun ...?
Who is he? (그는 누구입니까?) He is Tom. (그는 톰입니다.)	Whose skirt is this? (이것은 누구의 스커트입니까?) It is Jane's skirt. (그것은 제인의 스커트입니다.)
Who are they? (그들은 누구입니까?) They are Susan and Karen. (그들은 수잔과 카렌입니다.)	Whose glasses are they? (그것은 누구의 안경입니까?) They are Mark's glasses. (그것은 마크의 안경입니다.)

A **Read and check.**

1 Who are they? ✓
  Whose are they? ☐

2 Who dog is it? ☐
  Whose dog is it? ☐

3 Whose gloves are they? ☐
  Who gloves are they? ☐

4 Who is she? ☐
  Whose is she? ☐

5 Who are you? ☐
  Whose are you? ☐

6 Who pencil is it? ☐
  Whose pencil is it? ☐

1 __Whose__ books are they? •

• It is Brian's pen.

2 _____ is he? •

• They are Amy and Robert.

3 _____ pen is it? •

• She is Mary.

4 _____ are they? •

• They are Judy's books.

5 _____ is she? •

• He is Michael.

C Look and write.

1

_____ _____ you?

I am James.

2

_____ _____ _____ it?

It is Tracy's hat.

3

_____ _____ she?

She is Helen.

4

_____ _____ _____ it?

It is Andy's ball.

5

_____ _____ they?

They are my parents.

6

_____ _____ _____ they?

They are my pants.

D Read and unscramble.

1 [is] [it?] [coat] [Whose]

→ ___Whose coat is it?_____

2 [he?] [Who] [is]

→ _____

3 [Whose] [they?] [socks] [are]

→ _____

4 [Who] [they?] [are]

→ _____

5 [is] [Whose] [it?] [car]

→ _____

6 [you?] [Who] [are]

→ _____

E Read and correct.

1 Is who she?   → ___Who is she?_____

2 Dress whose is it?   → _____

3 Whose shoe are they? → _____

4 Who they are?   → _____

5 Whose shirt it is?   → _____

6 Whose erasers is it? → _____

When / Where

GRAMMAR POINT

의문사 When

- 의문사 when은 시간을 물을 때 사용하고, '언제'라고 해석합니다.
- be동사와 함께 쓰일 경우 When + be동사 + 주어? 순으로 씁니다.
- 일반동사와 함께 쓰일 경우 When + do/does + 주어 + 동사원형? 순으로 씁니다.

의문사 Where

- 의문사 where는 장소나 방향에 관해 물을 때 사용하고, '어디에'라고 해석합니다.
- be동사와 함께 쓰일 경우 Where + be동사 + 주어? 순으로 씁니다.
- 일반동사와 함께 쓰일 경우 Where + do/does + 주어 + 동사원형? 순으로 씁니다.

When ...?	Where ...?
When is your birthday? (당신은 생일이 언제입니까?) It is on April 20. (4월 20일입니다.)	Where are you? (당신은 어디에 있습니까?) I am in the kitchen. (저는 부엌에 있습니다.)
When do you go to bed? (당신은 언제 잠자리에 듭니까?) I go to bed at 10 o'clock. (저는 10시에 잠자리에 듭니다.)	Where does he go? (그는 어디에 갑니까?) He goes to school. (그는 학교에 갑니다.)

A Read and match.

1 When is the party? •

2 Where is he? •

3 When do you watch TV? •

4 Where does she study? •

• We watch TV at night.

• He is at school.

• It is on Saturday.

• She studies at home.

B Read and write.

1 <u>When</u> <u>is</u> Halloween? It is October 31.

2 _____ _____ they? They are in the classroom.

3 _____ _____ he eat lunch? He eats lunch at 12 o'clock.

4 _____ _____ you ride a bike? I ride a bike at the park.

5 _____ _____ she read a book? She reads a book at the library.

6 _____ _____ they go to school? They go to school at 8 o'clock.

C Look and write.

Kelly's Weekly Schedule

September 09

Sun 05	go to church
Mon 06	
Tue 07	Father's birthday
Wed 08	meet Edward at the park
Thu 09	
Fri 10	clean my room
Sat 11	*My birthday have a birthday party Tat home

1 <u>Where</u> <u>does</u> Kelly go on Sunday?
She goes to church.

2 _____ _____ her father's birthday?
It is on Tuesday.

3 _____ _____ she meet Edward?
She meets him at the park.

4 _____ _____ she clean her room?
She cleans her room on Friday.

5 _____ _____ her birthday?
It is on Saturday.

6 _____ _____ she have a birthday party?
She has a birthday party at her home.

D Read and unscramble.

1 [she?] [Where] [is]

→ Where is she?

2 [does] [go swimming?] [When] [he]

→ _____

3 [they] [do] [play soccer?] [Where]

→ _____

4 [is] [Christmas?] [When]

→ _____

5 [Where] [fly a kite?] [does] [she]

→ _____

6 [do] [When] [they] [come home?]

→ _____

E Read and correct.

1 When does he studies English? → When does he study English?

2 Are where you? → _____

3 Do when they play the piano? → _____

4 Where is she watch a movie? → _____

5 Is when Jane's birthday? → _____

6 Where do they lives? → _____

UNIT 23 How / How Old

GRAMMAR PoINT

의문사 How

- 의문사 how는 상태, 수단, 방법을 물을 때 사용하고, '어떻게'라고 해석합니다.
- be동사와 함께 쓰일 경우 How + be동사 + 주어? 순으로 씁니다.
- 일반동사와 함께 쓰일 경우 How + do/does + 주어 + 동사원형? 순으로 씁니다.
- how가 형용사와 결합하여 쓰일 경우 '얼마나'로 해석합니다.
- how가 형용사와 결합하여 be동사와 함께 쓰일 경우 How + 형용사 + be동사 + 주어? 순으로 씁니다.
- how가 형용사와 결합하여 일반동사와 함께 쓰일 경우 How + 형용사 + do/does + 주어 + 동사원형? 순으로 씁니다.

How ...?	How + Adjective ...?
How are you? (당신은 기분이 어때요?) I am fine. (저는 좋아요.)	How old is he? (그는 몇 살입니까?) He is ten years old. (그는 열 살입니다.)
How do you go to school? (당신은 학교에 어떻게 갑니까?) I go to school by bus. (저는 버스를 타고 학교에 갑니다.)	How many pens does she have? (그녀는 펜을 몇 자루 가지고 있습니까?) She has twelve pens. (그녀는 펜을 12자루 가지고 있습니다.)

A Read and circle.

1 (How)I How old are they?   They are sick.

2 How I How tall is the weather?   It is rainy.

3 How many I much juice is there?   There is a lot of juice.

4 How many I much cars are there?   There are a lot of cars.

5 How do I Do how you get there?   I get there by bus.

6 Does how I How does she come here?   She comes here on foot.

B Read and write.

1 __How__ __many__ apples are there?   There are five apples.

2 _____ _____ water does she have?   She has some water.

3 _____ _____ they go to school?   They go to school by bike.

4 _____ _____ you?   I am fine.

5 _____ _____ is he?   He is twelve years old.

C Look and write.

How	How old	How many	How much

1
__How__ do they get there?
They get there by bus.

2
_____ is she?
She is sad.

3
_____ _____ are you?
I am eleven years old.

4
_____ _____ bread is there?
There is a lot of bread.

5
_____ _____ pets do you have?
I have two pets.

6
_____ does he go to America?
He goes to America by airplane.

D Read and unscramble.

1 is | How | he?

    ➡ How is he?

2 . you | do | go to work? | How

    ➡ _____

3 do | How many | have? | you | pencils

    ➡ _____

4 there? | sugar | is | How much

    ➡ _____

5 is | she? | How old

    ➡ _____

6 How tall | they? | are

    ➡ _____

E Read and correct.

1 Do how they get there?   ➡ How do they get there?

2 Old how is he?   ➡ _____

3 How many book do you have? ➡ _____

4 How much milks is there?   ➡ _____

5 How tall you are?   ➡ _____

6 How does she feels?   ➡ _____

GRAMMAR POINT

의문사 Why

● 의문사 why는 이유를 물을 때 사용하고, '왜'라고 해석합니다.
● be동사와 함께 쓰일 경우 Why + be동사 + 주어 ...? 순으로 씁니다.
● 일반동사와 함께 쓰일 경우 Why + do/does + 주어 + 동사원형 ...? 순으로 씁니다.
● 접속사 because를 사용해서 대답합니다.

Question	Answer
Why are you happy? (당신은 왜 행복합니까?) Why is he late? (그는 왜 늦었습니까?)	I am happy because today is my birthday. (저는 오늘 제 생일이라 행복합니다.) He is late because he missed the bus. (그는 버스를 놓쳐서 늦었습니다.)
Why do they stay at home? (그들은 왜 집에 머물러 있습니까?) Why does she study English? (그녀는 왜 영어를 열심히 공부합니까?)	They stay at home because it is rainy. (그들은 비가 와서 집에 머물러 있습니다.) She studies English because she likes it. (그녀는 영어를 좋아해서 열심히 공부합니다.)

A Read and circle.

1 (Why I What) are you busy?

2 Why I What does he like ice cream?

3 Why I Whose is she thirsty?

4 Why do I does they stay up late?

5 Why do I does he go to the hospital?

6 Why do I does they invite their friends?

B **Read and write.**

1 ___Why___ ___do___ they like Tom? `d`

2 _____ _____ you late? `☐`

3 _____ _____ he buy flowers? `☐`

4 _____ _____ she happy? `☐`

> ⓐ He buys flowers because his mother likes them.
> ⓑ I am late because I missed the bus.
> ⓒ She is happy because she got a present.
> ⓓ They like Tom because he is kind.

C **Look and write.**

1

___Why___ ___is___ he thirsty?
He is thirsty because he is running.

2

_____ _____ she cry?
She cries because she is hungry.

3

_____ _____ they stay at home?
They stay at home because it is rainy.

4

_____ _____ you run to school?
I run to school because I am late.

5

_____ _____ you full?
I am full because I ate a lot of pizza.

D Read and unscramble.

1 [you] [are] [tired?] [Why]

→ _Why are you tired?_

2 [go] [Why] [he] [there?] [does]

→ _____

3 [is] [angry?] [Why] [she]

→ _____

4 [Why] [exercise?] [they] [do]

→ _____

5 [they] [are] [in the garden?] [Why]

→ _____

6 [does] [Why] [clean] [she] [her room?]

→ _____

E Read and correct.

1 Why he is sick?   → _Why is he sick?_____

2 Do why you get up early? → _____

3 Are why they at the park? → _____

4 Why does she eats chocolate? → _____

5 Does why it bark?   → _____

6 Why you are hungry?   → _____

Review VI — Units 20-24

A Read, write, and match.

> What   Who   Where   ~~When~~   How   Why

1 __When__ is your birthday? •   • I am in the living room.

2 _____ does he get there? •   • He gets there by bus.

3 _____ are you? •   • It is on May 14.

4 _____ are they? •   • He is sad because his cat is sick.

5 _____ does she like? •   • They are my parents.

6 _____ is he sad? •   • She likes apples.

B Read and write.

> What   How   Whose

1 __Whose__ shoes are they?   They are Jane's shoes.

2 _____ much cheese do you have?   I have a lot of cheese.

3 _____ sport does he like?   He likes soccer.

4 _____ tall is she?   She is 160cm tall.

5 _____ cap is it?   It is Michael's cap.

6 _____ color do they like?   They like pink.

C **Read, circle, and write.**

1 ___Where___ are my books? They are on the desk.
    ⓐ Who   ⓑ How   ©Where

2 _____ is she? She is Mary.
    ⓐ Who   ⓑ Whose   ⓒ Why

3 _____ do you like roses? I like roses because they are pretty.
    ⓐ What   ⓑ Why   ⓒ Where

4 _____ is Valentine's Day? It is on February 14.
    ⓐ When   ⓑ How many   ⓒ Where

5 _____ do you go to school? I go to school on foot.
    ⓐ When   ⓑ Why   ⓒ How

6 _____ umbrella is it? It is Katie's umbrella.
    ⓐ Who   ⓑ Whose   ⓒ What

7 _____ color do you like? I like red.
    ⓐ Who   ⓑ Whose   ⓒ What

8 Why are you tired? I am tired _____ I didn't sleep well.
    ⓐ always   ⓑ because   ⓒ early

9 _____ pencils are there? There are ten pencils.
    ⓐ How much   ⓑ How many   ⓒ What

10 _____ is your brother? He is twelve years old.
    ⓐ How old   ⓑ How many   ⓒ How much

Written by E2K
Illustrated by Kyowajin Illust

First published January 2013
4th printing November 2023

Publisher: Kyudo Chung
Editors: Mija Cho, Jungwon Min, Mikyoung Kim, Genie Jeong
Designers: Soonam Park, D#
Cover Design: Eunhee Lee, Gyobin Kim

Published and distributed by Happy House, an imprint of DARAKWON, Inc.
Darakwon Bldg., 211 Munbal-ro, Paju-si, Gyeonggi-do, 10881, Republic of Korea
Tel: 82-2-736-2031(Ext. 250)   **Fax:** 82-2-732-2037   **Homepage:** www.ihappyhouse.co.kr

ISBN: 978-89-6653-079-3   63740